Echoes

Also by Robert Creeley

POETRY

For Love • *Words* • *The Charm* • *Pieces*
A Day Book • *Hello: A Journal* • *Later*
Collected Poems 1945–1975 • *Mirrors*
Memory Gardens • *Selected Poems*
Windows

FICTION

The Gold Diggers • *The Island*
Presences • *Mabel: A Story*
Collected Prose

DRAMA

Listen

ESSAYS

A Quick Graph: Collected Notes & Essays
Was That a Real Poem & Other Essays
Collected Essays
Autobiography
Tales Out of School

ANTHOLOGIES AND SELECTIONS

The Black Mountain Review 1954–1957
New American Story (with Donald M. Allen)
The New Writing in the U.S.A. (with Donald M. Allen)
Selected Writings of Charles Olson
Whitman: Selected Poems
The Essential Burns
Charles Olson, *Selected Poems*

Robert Creeley

Echoes

A NEW DIRECTIONS BOOK

Acknowledgments: Grateful acknowledgment is made to the editors and pub-
lishers of magazines in which some of the poems in this book first appeared:
*American Poetry Review, Arshile, Beloit Poetry Journal, Bombay Gin, Die Young,
Fishers, Gas, Grand Street, The Harvard Review, Lilt, lyric&, Michigan Quarterly
Review, Notus, o·blēk, Poetry New York, Sagetrieb, Scarlet, :that:, Wallace Stevens
Journal, West Coast Lines.* Thanks too to the publishers of books and pamphlets
in which many of the poems also appeared: *Alex Katz* (Marlborough, 1991),
Dutch Boy (Living Batch Bookstore, 1993), *Gnomic Verses* (Zasterle Press, 1992),
Have a Heart (Limberlost Press, 1990), *It* (Bischofberger, 1989), *The Old Days*
(Ambrosia Press, 1991), *Parts,* with mezzotints by Susan Rothenberg (Lime-
stone Press, 1994), *Raging Like a Fire: A Celebration of Irving Layton* (Vehicule
Press, 1993), The *Scope of Words* (Peter Land, 1991), *WPFW89.3FM Poetry
Anthology* (The Bunny and the Crocodile Press, 1992). Thanks as well to Ken
and Ann Mikolowski's Alternative Press for its printing of the postcard
"Moral," to Elizabeth Robinson for the broadside "Death" and "Eyes," and to
Ray DiPalma for the broadside "Here and Now" in the *Stele* series. Finally, a
number of poems were prompted by a collaboration with the artist Cletus
Johnson, among them those collected as *Gnomic Verses.* Exhibitions of these
works were held at the Leo Castelli Gallery in New York, October 1990, and
at the Nina Freudenheim Gallery in Buffalo, April 1991.

Manufactured in the United States of America
New Directions Books are printed on acid-free paper.
First published clothbound by New Directions in 1994.
Published simultaneously in Canada by Penguin Books Canada Limited

Library of Congress Cataloging-in-Publication Data

Creeley, Robert, 1926–
   Echoes / Robert Creeley.
     p.   cm.
   Includes index.
   ISBN 0–8112–1263–7
   I. Title.
PS3505.R43E27 1994
811'.54—dc20

93–46674
CIP

New Directions Books are published for James Laughlin
by New Directions Publishing Corporation,
80 Eighth Avenue, New York 10011

Contents

for Pen, Will and Hannah

...Sea, hill and wood,
This populous village! Sea, and hill, and wood,
With all the numberless goings on of life,
Inaudible as dreams! the thin-blue flame
Lies on my low-burnt fire, and quivers not;
Only that film, which fluttered on the grate,
Still flutters there, the sole unquiet thing.
Methinks, its motion in this hush of nature
Gives it dim sympathies with me who live,
Making it a companionable form,
Whose puny flaps and freaks the idling Spirit
By its own moods interprets, every where
Echo or mirror seeking of itself,
And makes a toy of Thought.

S. T. Coleridge, "Frost at Midnight"

1

MY NEW MEXICO

for Gus Blaisdell

Edge of door's window
sun against
flat side adobe,
yellowed brown—

A blue lifting morning,
miles of spaced echo,
time here plunged
backward, backward—

I see shadowed leaf
on window frame green,
close plant's growth,
weathered fence slats—

All passage explicit,
the veins, hands,
lined faces crease,
determined—

Oh sun! Three years,
when I came first,
it had shone unblinking,
sky vast aching blue—

The sharpness of each
shift the pleasure,
pain, of particulars—
All inside gone out.

Sing me a song
makes beat specific,
takes the sharp air,
echoes this silence.

BRICK

Have I bricked up unbricked what
perspective hole break of eye
seen what glowing place what
flower so close grows from a
tiny brown seed or was it what
I wanted this after imaged green
round sun faints under blue sky
or outer space that place no
one knows but for this echo of
sketched in color the stems of
the voluptuous flowers patient
myself inside looking still out.

BOWL

He comes she comes carrying carrying
a flower an intense interest a color
curious placed in an outer an inner
ring of rounded spaces of color it
looked this way they say it was here
and there it was it opened opens color
it sees itself seen faithful to echo
more than all or was the green seeming
back of it fragile shoots a way it was
yellow banded together zigzagged across
as a box for it wants to touch touches
opens at the edges a flower in a bowl.

SHADOW

There is a shadow
to intention a place
it comes through and
is itself each stasis
of its mindedness ex-
plicit walled into
semblance it is a
seemingly living place
it wants it fades it
comes and goes it puts
a yellow flower in a pot
in a circle and looks.

FIGURE OF FUN

Blue dressed aged blonde
person with pin left
lapel hair bulged to
triangular contained wide
blue grey eyed now
authority prime minister
of aged realm this
hallowed hollowed ground
lapped round with salted water
under which a tunnel runs
to far off France and history
once comfortably avoided.

WALDOBORO EVE

Trees haze in the fog coming in,
late afternoon sun still catches the stones.

Dog's waiting to be fed by the empty sink,
I hear the people shift in their rooms.

That's all finally there is to think.
Now comes night with the moon and the stars.

OLD

Framed roof slope from tower's window
out to grey wet field with green growth,
edge again of midfield hedgerow and trees beyond,
the tugging familiar, the fading off fogged distance—

Are these memories already?
Does it seem to me I see what's there.
Have I particulars still to report,
is my body myself only?

Hear the cricket, the keening slight
sound of insect, the whirring of started
vacuum cleaner, television's faint voices now
down below. Here is world.

OLD WORDS

The peculiar *fuck it*
cunt shit violence
of a past learned in
school all words only
one by one first heard
never forgotten as recall
head or heart vagaries
a dusk now so early
in the afternoon the wet
feel of days socks touch
of things said to me
forever please *fuck me.*

TRANSLATION

You have all the time been
here if not seen, not thought
of as present, for when I
looked I saw nothing, when
I looked again, you had
returned. This echo, sweet
spring, makes a human sound
you have no need of, facts
so precede, but you hear, you
hear it, must feel the intent
wetness, mushy. I melt again
into your ample presence.

SELF PORTRAIT

This face was detachable
as blurred head itself
lifted from old bookcover
library yielded a faded
years ago image graced
now newspaper's rushed
impression static glossed
sentiment "life" a few hours
more to "live" till wrapped
tight round fresh loaf delivered
come home eaten comes to rest
on yesterday's garbage.

HERE AGAIN

He was walking
toward the other in-
viting him for-
ward now with an
eager antici-
pation he could rec-
ognize if not al-
together trust him-
self with any-
one else still
waiting also
to be met.

ECHO

Entire memory
hangs tree
in mind to see
a bird be—

but now puts stutter
to work, shutters
the windows, shudders,
sits and mutters—

because can't
go back, still
can't get
out. Still can't.

PURE

Why is it *pure*
so defeats, makes
simple possibility
cringe in opposition—

That bubbling, mingled
shit with water
lifted from bathtub's
drain hole's no

stranger to me,
nor ever in mind
blurred image, words
won't say what's

asked of them. I
think the world I think,
wipe my relentless ass,
wash hands under faucet.

EYES

I hadn't noticed that
building front had narrow
arrowlike division going
up it the stairwell at
top a crest like spearpoint
red roofed it glistens
with rain the top sharply
drawn horizontal roof edge lets
sky back there be a faint
blue a fainter white light
growing longer now higher
going off out of sight.

SOME

You have not simply
insisted on yourself
nor argued
the irrelevance

of any one else. You
have always wanted
to be friends, to be
one of many.

Persuaded
life even
in its largeness
might be brought

to care, you
tried to make it
care, humble, illiterate,
awkward gestured.

So you thought,
as inevitable age approached,
some loved you,
some.

You waited for
some wind
to lift, some
thing to happen,

proving it finally,
making sense more
than the literal,
still separate.

ECHO

White light blocked
impulse of repose like
Wouldn't you tell me
what you were doing   Couldn't
I go where you go   Faith
you kept secretly because it
had no other place to be   My
eyeball's simple hole wherein
'the gold gathered the
glow around it'   All you
said you wanted fainted
All the ways to say   No

THERE

Seeming act
of thought's
gagging

insight out
there's spasmodic
patience a wreck

car's hauled
now away
another day's

gone to hell
you know like
hangs out.

HERE ONLY

Why does it cry so much
facing its determined despair—
As woman locked in cage—
child—or eyes only left to look—
Why—   What wanted—   Why is it
this way or that way thrashes
stubborn only in its absence—
It was never there—was only
here to be itself—here only this
one chance to be—   Cannot live
except it finds a place given—
Open to itself only as any—

IT

Nothing there
in absence as,
unfelt, it
repeated itself—

I saw it,
felt it,
wanted
to belt it—

Oh love, you
watch, you
are so
"patient"—

Or what
word makes my
malice
more.

DEATH

Unlet things
static dying
die in common
pieces less
crescendo
be it simple
complex death
a physical
world again un-
ended unbegun to
any other world
be this one.

HERE AND NOW

Never other than this unless
is counted sudden, demanded
sense of falling or a loud,
inexplicable yell just back
of ears, or if the tangible
seeming world rears up dis-
torted, bites hands that would
feed it, can feel no agreeable
sensation in the subject's hard-
ly learned vocabulary of social
moves, agreements, mores—
then up shit creek sans paddle.

ABSTRACT

The inertia unexpected of
particular reference, it
wasn't where you said it
would be, where you looked
wasn't where it was! What
fact of common world is
presumed common? The
objectifying death of all
human person, the ground?
There you are and I look
to see you still, all
the distance still implacable.

THE CUP

Who had thought
echo precedent,

shadow the seen
thing, action

reflective—
whose thought was

consequential,
itself an act, a

walking round rim
to see what's within.

CHAIN

Had they told you, you
were "four or more cells
joined end to end," the Latin,
catena, "a chain," the loop,
the running leap to actual
heaven spills at my stunned
feet, pours out the imprison-
ing threads of genesis,
oh light beaded necklace,
chain round my neck, my
inexorably bound birth, the sweet
closed curve of fading life?

EAST STREET

Sense of the present
world out window, eye's
blurred testament

to "St Francis Xavier's
School," red brick
and grey cornices,

the snow, day old,
like thin, curdled milk,
God's will high

above on cross
at church top over
embedded small arches

and close, tiled
roof. The cars
parked, the accelerating

motor of one
goes by, the substantial
old birch, this

closer look—
path Dennis shoveled—
distraction of all report.

BAROQUE

Would you live your life spectrum
of fly sealed in amber block's
walk the patient fixed window see
days a measure of tired time a
last minute thought of whatever not
now remembered lift up sit down
then be reminded the dog is your
paradigm seven years to one all
reckoned think out muse on be sud-
denly outside the skin standing
upright pimpled distinction chilled
independence found finally only one?

FOR NOTHING ELSE

For nothing else,
this for love

for what other
one is this

for love once
was and is

for love,
for love.

PARTS

for Susan Rothenberg

HUMAN LEG GOAT LEG

Which the way echoed
previous cloven-hoofed
dark field faint formed
those *goat men leading her*
in physical earth's spring
jumps one-legged parallel
long walked thinned out
to sparse grounded skin
bones of what scale say
now goat transforms man
then man goat become
and dances dances?

SNAKE FISH BIRD

Archaic evolving thing
in all surface all beginning
not hair or any seeming simple
extension bring to mind pattern
of woven wetnesses waste a streak
of wonder of evil tokens the underneath
beside ground's depths spoken
low in sight soundless in height
look past reflection see the light
flash of finned ripple wing
this ancient *Fellow* follow
to weather, to water, to earth.

HORSE LEG DOG HEAD

Its mute uncute cutoff
inconsequent eye slot
centuries' habits accumulate
barks the determined dog
beside horse the leg the
walking length the patent
patient slight bent limb
long fetlock faith faint
included instructions placed
aside gone all to vacant
grass placed patiently thus
foot's function mind's trust.

DOG LEG WHEEL

Four to the round
repetitive inexorable
sound the wheel the whine
the wishes of dogs
that the world be real
that masters feel
that bones be found
somewhere in the black ground
in front or in back
before and behind
hub for a head bark's
a long way back. And on

GOAT'S EYE

Eye hole's peculiar framed
see you, want you, think
of eye out, lost last sight,

past goat thoughts, what
was it, when or why—
Or if still the stiff
hair, musk, the way
eye looks out, black
line contracted, head's skull
unstudied, steady,
it led to lust, follows
its own way down to dust.

DOG HEAD WITH RABBIT LEG

Break the elliptical
make the face deadpan tell
nothing to it smile for the
camera lie down and roll over
be in complex pieces for once
you ran the good race broke
down and what's left you
least of all can understand.
It was cold. It was hard.
Dogs barked. Rabbits ran.
It comes to such end,
friend. Such is being dead.

DOG HEAD WITH CRESCENT MOON

Harvested this head's
a manifest of place the
firmament's fundament.
Overhead sky's black night
in lieu of echoed moon
seems sounding out
a crescent crescendo
for a dog's life.

Barked bones soft
mouth's brought home
the arc again the light.
Waits patient for reward.

BIRD AND CALF

Peculiar patience is death
like an envelope a flap
a postulate you'd left a
space where it was and it
has gathered the outside
of its body in or just
flopped down dropped all
alternative forever waiting
for the plummeting streak
gets closer closer and
the god who cleans up things
puts death to work.

HORSES' BREATH

Had never known blue air's
faded fascination had never
seen or went anywhere never
was a horse unridden but on
one proverbial frosty morning
whilst going to the kitchen
I thought of our lives' opaque
addiction to distances to
all the endless riders etched
on those faint horizons and
nuzzled the mere idea of you—
swapped breath. *Oh love, be true!*

2

WHITE FENCE/WHITE FENCE

(for Paul Strand's photograph "White Fence")

Particularizing "White
Fence" beyond which
the seeming

echoes of barn, house,
bright light flat
on foursquare

far building while
in closer view shades
darken the faint ground.

Yet *fence* as
image or word,
white or black, or

where place the person,
the absent,
in this ring of focus?

I come closer, see
in *there* the
wistful security,

all in apparent place,
the resonant design, diamond,
the *dark/light,*

the way all plays to pattern,
the longed for world
of common facts.

Then this *fence* again,
as if pasted on,
pushes out and across,

a static, determined
progress of detailing
edges, *American,* an

odd reason so forced
to be seen. It
cannot accommodate,

cannot let get past,
unaffected, any, *must* be
"White Fence."

EAST STREET AGAIN

for Carl Rakosi

The tree stands clear in the weather
by the telephone pole, its stiff brother.
Hard to think which is the better,
given living is what we're here for
and that one's soon dead no matter.
Neither people nor trees live forever.
But it's a dumb thought, lacking other.
Only this passing faint snow now for tether—
mind's deadness, emptiness for pleasure—
if such a flat, faint echo can be measure.
So much is forgotten no matter.
You do what you can do, no better.

SONNETS

for Keith and Rosmarie

Come round again the banal
belligerence almost a
flatulent echo of times
when still young the Sino
etc conflict starvation lists
of people without work or place
world so opaque and desperate
no one wanted even to
go outside to play even
with Harry Buddy who hit
me who I hit stood slugging
while they egged us on.

•

While ignorant armies clash
bash while on the motorway
traffic backed up while they
stand screaming at each other
while they have superior
armaments so wage just
war while it all provokes
excuses alternatives money
time wasted go tell it
on the town dump deadend
avoidance of all you might
have lived with once.

•

Someone told me to stand
up to whoever pushed me

down when talking walking
hand on friend's simple
pleasures thus abound when
one has fun with one
another said surrogate
God and planted lettuce
asparagus had horses cows
the farm down the road
the ground I grew up
on unwon unending.

•

I'd take all the learned
manner of rational un-
derstanding away leave
the table to stand on
its own legs the plates
to stick there the food
for who wants it the places
obvious and ample and
even in mind think it
could be other than an
argument a twisting
away tormented unless.

•

Me is finally unable having
as all seem to ended with
lost chances happily enough
missed the boat took them
all to hell on a whim
went over whatever precipice
but no luck just stupid
preoccupation common

fear of being overly hurt
by the brutal exigencies were
what pushed and pulled
me too to common cause.

.

So being old and wise and
unwanted left over from
teeth wearing hands wearing
feet wearing head wearing
clothes I put on take now
off and sleep or not or sit
this afternoon morning night
time's patterns look up at
stars overhead there what
do they mean but how useless
all violence how far away you
are from what you want.

.

Some people you just
know and recognize,
whether a need or fact,
a disposition at that
moment is placed,
you're home, a light
is in that simple
window forever—   As if
people had otherwise always
to be introduced, told
you're ok—   But here
you're home, so longed
for, so curiously
without question found.

OTHER

Having begun in thought there
in that factual embodied wonder
what was lost in the emptied lovers
patience and mind I first felt there
wondered again and again what for
myself so meager and finally singular
despite all issued therefrom whether
sister or mother or brother and father
come to love's emptied place too late
to feel it again see again first there
all the peculiar wet tenderness the care
of her for whom to be other was first fate.

BODY

Slope of it,
hope of it—
echoes faded,
what waited

up late inside
old desires
saw through
the screwed importunities.

This regret?
Nothing's left.
Skin's old,
story's told—

but still touch,
selfed body,
wants other,
another mother

to him, her
insistent "sin"
he lets in
to hold him.

Selfish bastard,
headless catastrophe.
Sans tits, cunt,
wholly blunt—

fucked it up,
roof top, loving cup,
sweatered room,
old love's tune.

Age dies old,
both men and women cold,
hold at last no one,
die alone.

Body lasts forever,
pointless conduit,
floods in its fever,
so issues others parturient.

Through legs wide,
from common hole site,
aching information's dumb tide
rides to the far side.

"YOU WERE NEVER LOVELIER..."

for Cletus

Inside that insistence—
small recompense—   Persistence—
No sense in witless
thoughtlessness, no one

has aptitude for waiting—
hating, staying away later,
alone, left over, saw
them all going

without her (him), wanted
one for him (her)self, left
on the shelf, "them" become
fact of final indifference—

The theme is thoughtlessness,
the mind's openness, the
head's large holes, the gaps
in apparent thinking. So that

amorphic trucks drive through
you, mere, mired, if unmoved,
agency, left by the proposed "they"
to stay, alone of all that was.

The world is, or seems, entirely
an aggression, a running over, an
impossible conjunct of misfits
crash about, hurting one another.

No names please, no no one or someone.
Say goodbye to the nonexistent—never

having lived again or ever, mindless—
trucks, holes, clouds, call them—

those sounds of shapes in tides of space—
pillaging weather, shifting about one
or two or simply several again, an issue
only of surmise, a surprise of

sunset or sunrise, a day or two can't
think about or move out, or be again certain,
be about one's own business, be vanity's own simpleton,
simply, *You Were Never Lovelier...*

REFLECTION

It must be low key
breeze blowing through
room's emptiness is
something to think of—

but not enough
punch, pain enough,
despair to make
all else fade out—

This morning, that
morning? Another ample
day in the diminishing
possibility, the

reflective reality
alters to place
in specific place
what can't get past.

THE OLD DAYS

Implicit echo of the
seemingly friendly
face and grace as well
to be still said. Go to hell

(or heaven), old American
saying—   My sister's friends
are affectionate people,
and also seemingly real.

Can I calculate—as to say,
can I still stay up late
enough to catch Santa Claus or
New Year's, are the small, still

tenets of truth still observable—
And how is your mother? Dead, sir,
these less than twenty years.
The voice echoes the way it was—

And if I am mistaken, sir.
If I am thought in error, was the error
intentional, did I mean to confuse you.
Were the great waves of myriad voices too

much of enough—   You remember Cocteau's *A little
too much is enough for me*—   Tits were beautiful—
bubbles of unstable flesh, pure, tilting pleasure.
You cannot finally abjure beauty

nor can you simply live without it—
reflective, beating your meat, unspeakable,
light headed with loneliness. Oh to be old
enough, fall down the stairs, break everything—

One often did but in such company
was heaven—   Breath, arms, eyes,
and consummate softness—   Breathing softness,
moist, simply conjoining softness, like a pillow.

No man is an island, no woman a pillow—
Nobody's anything anymore. Was it Pound
who said, *The way out is via the door*—
Do they say that anymore—

Do I hear what I hear. Then where
are the snows of yesteryear,
the face that sank a thousand ships,
all that comforting, nostalgic stuff

we used to hear. Sitting in company
with others, I look at the backs
of my hands, see slightly mottled,
swollen flesh, hear difficultly

through many voices—see a blur.
Yet you were, you are here—
If I am a fool in love,
you'll never leave me now.

YOUR

One sided
battering ramm'd
negligible asset
carnal friend—

Patience's provision
test of time
nothing ventured
nothing gained—

In the fat doldrums
of innocent aging
I sat waiting—
Thank god you came.

GNOMIC VERSES

LOOP

Down the road Up the hill Into the house
Over the wall Under the bed After the fact
By the way Out of the woods Behind the times
In front of the door Between the lines Along the path

ECHO

In the way it was in the street
it was in the back it was
in the house it was in the room
it was in the dark it was

FAT FATE

Be at That this
Come as If when
Stay or Soon then
Ever happen It will

LOOK

Particular pleasures weather measures or
Dimestore delights faced with such sights.

HERE

Outstretched innocence
Implacable distance
Lend me a hand
See if it reaches

TIME

Of right Of wrong Of up Of down
Of who Of how Of when Of one
Of then Of if Of in Of out
Of feel Of friend Of it Of now

MORAL

Now the inevitable
As in tales of woe
The inexorable toll
It takes, it takes.

EAT

Head on backwards
Face front neck's
Pivot bunched flesh
Drops jowled brunch.

TOFFEE

Little bit patted pulled
Stretched set let cool.

CASE

Whenas To for
If where From in
Past place Stated want
Gain granted Planned or

HAVE A HEART

Have heart Find head
Feel pattern Be wed
Smell water See sand
Oh boy Ain't life grand

OH OH

Now and then
Here and there
Everywhere
On and on

WINTER

Season's upon us
Weather alarms us
Snow riot peace
Leaves struck fist

DUTY

Let little Linda allow litigation
Foster faith's fantasy famously
And answer all apt allegations
Handmake Harold's homework handsomely

GOTCHA

Passion's particulars
Steamy hands

Unwashed warmth
One night stands

WEST ACTON SUMMER

Cat's rats, Mother's brother
Vacation's patience, loud clouds
Fields far, seize trees
School's rules, friends tend
Lawn's form, barn's beams
Hay's daze, swallows follow
Sun's sunk, moon mends
Echo's ending, begin again

FAR

"Far be it from Harry to alter the sense of drama
inherent in the almighty tuxedo..."

"Far be it from Harry"
Sit next to Mary
See how the Other
Follows your Mother

PAT'S

Pat's place
Pattern's face
Aberrant fact
Changes that

FOUR'S

Four's forms
Back and forth
Feel way Hindside
Paper route Final chute

SENTENCES

Indefatigably alert when hit still hurt.
Whenever he significantly alters he falters.
Wondrous weather murmured mother.
Unforgettable twist in all such synthesis.
Impeccably particular you always were.
Laboriously enfeebled he still loved people.

WORDS

Driving to the expected
Place in mind in
Place of mind in
Driving to the expected

HERE

You have to reach
Out more it's
Farther away from
You it's here

DATA

Exoneration's face
Echoed distaste

Privileged repetition
Makeshift's decision—

•

Now and then
Behind time's
Emptied scene and
Memory's mistakes—

•

You are here
And there too
Being but one
Of you—

SCATTER

All that's left of coherence.

ECHO AGAIN

Statement keep talking
Train round bend over river into distance

DOOR

Everything's before you
were here.

SUMMER '38

Nubble's Light a sort
of bump I thought—
a round insistent
small place

not like this—
it was a bluff,
up on the edge
of the sea.

AIR

Lift up so you're
Floating out
Of your skin at
The edge but
Mostly up seeming
Free of the ground.

ECHOES

Think of the
Dance you could do
One legged man
Two legged woman.

THERE

Hard to be unaddressed—
Empty to reflection—
Take the road east—
Be where it is.

ECHOES

Sunrise always first—
That light—is it
Round the earth—what
Simple mindedness.

STAR

Where
It is
There
You are

•

Out there
In here
Now it is
Was also

•

Up where
It will be
And down
Again

•

No one
Point
To it
Ever

ECHO

Brutish recall
seems useless now
to us all.

But my teeth you said
were yellow
have stayed nonetheless.

It was your handsomeness
went sour, your
girlish insouciance,

one said.
Was being afraid
neurotic?

Did you talk of it.
Was the high cliff jumpable.
Enough enough?

Fifty years
have passed.
I look back,

while you stand here,
see you there, still
see you there.

THINKING OF WALLACE STEVENS

After so many years the familiar
seems even more strange, the hands

one was born with even more remote, the feet
worn to discordant abilities, face fainter.

I love, loved you, Esmeralda, darling Bill.
I liked the ambience of others, the clotted crowds.

Inside it was empty, at best a fountain in winter,
a sense of wasted, drab park, a battered nonentity.

Can I say the whole was my desire?
May I again reiterate my single purpose?

No one can know me better than myself,
whose almost ancient proximity grew soon tedious.

The joy was always to know it was the joy,
to make all acquiesce to one's preeminent premise.

The candle flickers in the quick, shifting wind.
It reads the weather wisely in the opened window.

So it is the dullness of mind one cannot live without,
this place returned to, this place that was never left.

A NOTE

I interrupt these poems to bring you some lately particular information, which is that such coherence or determining purpose as I presumed myself to have in a collection such as this (not very long ago at all) seems now absent. Thus I collect much as a magpie (in Duncan's engaging sense) all that attracts me. Be it said once again that writing is a pleasure. So I am not finally building roads or even thinking to persuade the reader of some conviction I myself hold dear. I am trying to practice an art, which has its own insistent authority and needs no other, however much it may, in fact, say. I had not really understood what the lone boy whistling in the graveyard was fact of. Now I listen more intently.

ALEX'S ART

Art's a peculiar division of labors—"a small town cat before he
    [joined the band"—
as if the whole seen world were then an echo

Of anyone's mind in a past tense of Arabs, say,
inventing tents in the early hours of meager history.

It is "an ever fixed mark," a parallel, "blue
suede persuasion," a thing out there beyond

Simple industries and all those sad captains thereof.
It is a place elsewhere, time enough, "please

Pass the bacon" again, oh finite, physical person.
Listen to the wonders of how it's been, or how it is

And will be, now as sky lifts the faint edge of morning in
    [yellowish grey tones,
as I hear nothing, as I listen again, brought into myself,

As all of it now tails back of me in flooded pockets,
as even the hum of the machine, call it, sings its persistent song—

As each so-called moment, each plunge and painful recovery
of breath echoes its precedent, its own so-called raison d'être,

Arch or meager, living or forgotten, here or finally there,
as it thinks the givens, feels around for place to put them down,

No metaphoric by-pass, no hands in pockets, no home alone,
no choice, nowhere to sit down. But what is immensely evident,

Even in each particular such as always that "where are the snows
    [of yesteryear,"

is why pay so painfully in advance for what can never be here
[now?

Look at it this way. You know those simple coordinates of A and
[B.
Add C, the comedian. Add X and Y. Add the apparent sun and
[simple sky.

Add everything and everyone you've ever known. Still empty?
[Still
only time enough to settle the bills, or try to, to be kind to the dog
[who waits?

Trees' edges defined more now as sun lifts, lifted, to higher point
[in far off space.
I see this world as a common picture, having among others two
[dimensions

As well as a presently pleasant odor like, say, fresh cut hay. I hear
[little,
given my ears are not working quite properly, and I have gone
[indoors

A long, long way down a tunnel to where my TV sits on a table,
and I sit before it, watching the news. All a world in mind, isn't it,

As we do or do not get the bad guys? I don't know. But I still can
[see,
and I look at you. The simple question still. Can you see me?

DUTCH BOY

I'd thought
boy caught stopped

dike's dripping water
with finger

put in hole
held it all back

oh hero
stayed steadfast

through night's black
sat waited

till dawn's light
when people came

repaired the leak
rescued

sad boy. But
now I see what

was the fact
he was stuck

not finger in hole was
but he could not

take it out
feared he'd be caught

be shamed
blamed

so sat
through the night

uncommonly distraught
in common fright.

FRAGMENT

Slight you lift.
Edge skin down.
Circle seen.
Places now found.

Featured face.
Hand in when.
Disposition.
Distrust.

3

FAINT FACES

I can't move
as formerly but
still keep
at it as the

ground cants
rising to manage
some incumbent
cloud of

reference left
years back
the tracks absent
events it

was part of
parting and
leaving still
here still there.

TIME

How long for the small yellow flowers
ride up from the grasses' bed,
seem patient in that place—

What's seen of all I see
for all I think of it—
but cannot wait, no, *cannot* wait.

The afternoon, a time, floats
round my head, a boat I float on,
sit on, sat on, still rehearse.

I seem the faded register, the misplaced camera,
the stuck, forgotten box, the unread book,
the rained on paper or the cat went out for good.

Nowhere I find it now or even
stable within the givens, thus comfortable to reason,
this sitting on a case, this fact sans face.

THIS HOUSE

Such familiar space
out there, the window
frame's locating

focus I could
walk holding
on to

through air from
here to there,
see it where

now fog's close
denseness floats
the hedgerow up

off apparent ground,
the crouched, faint
trees lifting up

from it, and more
close down
there in front

by roof's slope, down,
the stonewall's conjoining,
lax boulders sit,

years' comfortable pace
unreturned, placed
by deliberation and

limit make their
sprawled edge. Here
again inside

the world one thought of,
placed in this aged box
moved here from

family site
lost as us, time's
spinning confusions

are what
one holds on to.
Hold on, dear house,

'gainst the long hours
of emptiness, against
the wind's tearing force.

You are my mind
made particular,
my heart in its place.

THE ROAD

Whatever was else or less
or more or even
the sinister prospect
of nothing left,

not this was anticipated,
that there would be no one
even to speak of it.
Because all had passed over

to wherever they go.
Into the fiery furnace
to be burned to ash.
Into the ground,

into mouldering skin and bone
with mind the transient guest,
with the physical again dominant
in the dead flesh under the stones.

Was this the loved hand, the
mortal "hand still capable of grasping..."
Who could speak
to make death listen?

One grows older,
gets closer.
It's a long way home,
this last walking.

THE PLACE

Afternoon it changes
and lifts, the heavy
fog's gone and the wind

rides the field, the flowers,
to the far edge
beyond what's seen.

It's a dream
of something or
somewhere I'd been

or would be, a place
I had made
with you, marked out

with string
years ago. Hannah
and Will are

no longer those
children
simply defined.

Is it weather
like wind blows, and all
to the restless sea?

PERSONAL

"Urgent" what the message says.
First of all purposes.
The loss of place for porpoises.
Less use of detergents.

Lack luster linens.
Tables without chairs.
Passionate abilities given little leeway.
They never were.

Thirties a faded time.
Forties the chaos of combat.
Fifties lots of loneliness.
Sixties redemption.

I look at you.
You look at me.
We see.
We continue.

PARADE

Measure's inherent
in the weight,
the substance itself
the person.

How far, how
long, how high,
what's there
now and why.

Cries in the dark,
screams out,
silence,
throat's stuck.

Fist's a weak grip,
ears blotted with echoes,
mind fails focus
and's lost.

Feet first,
feet last,
what difference,
down or up.

You were the shape
I took in the dark.
You the me
apprehended.

Wonders!
Simple fools,
rulers, all of us
die too.

On the way
much happiness
of a day,
no looking back.

ONWARD

"We cannot give you any support
if we don't know who you are."

You cannot drive on this road
if you do not have a car.

I cannot sleep at night
if I won't go to bed.

They used to be my friends
but now they are dead.

ONE WAY

Oh I so
like the
avoidance
common

to patient
person stands
on curb waiting
to cross.

Why not run out
get clobbered truck
car or bus
busted

to bits
smiling even
in defeat
stay simple.

Such sizing up
of reality
whiff of reaction
you will not

walk far alone
already the crowd
is with you or else
right behind.

I see you
myself sit
down walk too
no different

just the patient
pace we keep
defeats us
in the street.

THE WORDSWORTHS

for Warren

The Wordsworths afoot
fresh fields' look

birds hop on gravestone
small lake beyond

up long dank road
Coleridge's home—

Out this window I see
a man turning hay

early sun's edge
strike the green hedge

a blue round of field flower
mark the fresh hour

high spike of mullein
look over walled stone—

House slope blacked roof
catches eye's proof

returns me to day
passed far away

Dorothy took note,
William wrote.

HERE

Seen right of head,
window's darkening outlook
to far field's slope
past green hedgerow.

Here, slanted lengthening
sun on back wall's
dancing shadows,
now comes night.

FIVE VARIATIONS ON "ELATION"

for Bill McClung

This sudden
uplift elation's
pride's brought out!

Even ambiguity's
haughtily exalted oh
rushed, raised spirit.

    •

Rushed unexpected my
heart leaps up when
I behold the sudden
as in the common.

    •

Curiously with pride
above common lot to walk,

to be lifted up
and out, exalted.

    •

His elation was brief?
Brought back to earth,

still for a time
it was otherwise.

    •

Faded but unforgotten
if down once
uplifted if unsure
once proud if
inside once out.

•

ECHO

Elation's ghost
dance echoes
little, leaves no
traces, counts
no number—

Wants from no
one privilege. Has
no pride by being it.
If then recognized,
needs no company.

What wind's echo,
uplifted spirit?
Archaic feelings
flood the body.
Ah! accomplished.

EDGES

for Pen's birthday (everyday)

Edges of the field, the blue flowers, the reddish wash of
the grasses, the cut green path up to the garden
plot overgrown with seedlings and weeds—

green first of all, but light, the cut of the sunlight
edges each shift of the vivid particulars, grown large
—even the stones large in their givens, the shadows massing

their bulk, and so seeing I could follow out to another
edge of the farther field, where trees are thick on the sky's
edge, thinking I am not simply a response to this, this light,

not just an agency sees and vaguely adumbrates, adds an
    [opinion.
There is no opinion for life, no word more or less general.
I had begun and returned, again and again, to find you finally,

felt it all gather, as here, to be a place again, and wanted to
shuck the husk of habits, to lift myself to you in this sunlight.
If it is age, then what does age matter? If it is older or younger,

what moment notes it? In this containment there cannot
be another place or time. It all lives by its being
here and now, this persistent pleasure, ache of promise, misery
    [of all that's lost.

Now as if this moment had somehow secured to itself a body,
had become you, just here and now, the wonders inseparable
in this sunlight, *here,* had come to me again.

BILLBOARDS

AGE

Walking on
the same
feet
birth

provided,
I is not
the simple
question

after all,
nor *you*
an interesting
answer.

MORAL

Practice
your humility
elsewhere
'cause it's just another

excuse for privilege,
another place not
another's, another
way you get to get.

BIG TIME

What you got
to kill now isn't

dead enough
already? Wait,

brother, it *dies*, it
no way can *live*
without you, it's
waiting in line.

ECHO

It was a thoughtful
sense of paced
consideration,
whatever the agenda

had prompted as
subject. "Here we
are," for example, or
"There they were"...

So all together now,
a deep breath, a
fond farewell.
Over.

TRUE OR FALSE

"One little
freckle
houses
bacteria

equal
to the population
of New York—"
You cannot

breath, scratch
or move
sans killing
what so

lives on you.
There are
no vacancies, no
rooms with a view.

DREAM

What's the truth
for except it
makes a place for
common entrances, an

old way home down
the street 'midst faces,
the sounds' flooding
poignance, the approach?

SKY

Now that the weather softens the
end of winter in the tips of
trees' buds grow lighter a yellow
air of lifting slight but persistent
warmth you walk past the street's
far corner with turbanlike color swathed
hat and broad multicolored shawl hangs
down over your trunklike blue cloth
coat with legs black dog's tugging
pull on leash's long cord I walk quickly
to catch up to you pulled equally by
your securing amplitude, blue love!

A BOOK

for Pam and Lew

A book of such
sweetness the
world attends
one after

another a found
explicit fondness
mends the tear
threads intercross

here where there
repairs a cluster
comes mitigates
irritation reads words.

A VIEW AT EVENING

Cut neat path out
to darkening
garden plot
old field's forgot.

Far hedge row's
growth goes
down the hill
where blurred

trees depend,
find an end
in distance
under dark clouds.

The upright space,
place, fades sight,
sees echoes,
green, green, green.

THIS ROOM

Each thing given
place in the pattern
rather find
place in mind

a diverse face
absent past
shelf of habits
bits pieces

eye lost then
love's mistakes
aunt's battered house
off foundation

children's recollection
tokens
look back
chipped broken

room goes on
dark winter's edge
now full with sun
pales the worn rug.

SINS

A hand's part,
mouth's open look,
foot beside
the long leg.

Away again.
Inside the house
open windows
look out.

It was fun.
Then it's gone.
Come again
some time.

TIME'S FIXED

Time's fixed
as ticking instrument,
else day's insistent
ending into

which one walks,
finds the door shut,
and once again
gets caught, gets caught.

A captive heart,
a head, a hand,
an ear, the empty bed
is here—

A dull, an
unresponding man
or woman dead
to plan or plot.

Between what was
and what might be
still seems to be
a life.

HEAVEN

Wherever they've
gone they're
not here
anymore

and all
they stood
for is empty
also.

ECHOES

In which the moment
just left reappears or
seems as if present
again its fact intact—

In which a willing
suspension of disbelief
alters not only the judgment
but all else equally—

In which the time passes
vertically goes up and
up to a higher place a
plane of singular clarity—

In which these painfully small
endings shreds of emptying
presence sheddings of seeming
person can at last be admitted.

ECHO

It was never
simple to wait,
to sit quiet.

Was there still
another way round,
a distance to go—

as if an echo
hung in
the air before

one was heard,
before a word
had been said.

What was love
and where
and how did one get there.

ECHO

The return of things
round the great
looping bend in the road

where you remember
stood in mind
greyed encumbrances

patient dead dog
long lost love
till chair's rocking

became roar
sitting static
end of vision

day seems held up
by white hands were
looking for what was

gone couldn't come
back what was with
it wouldn't come looking.

ECHO

for Eck

Find your way out
no doubt
or in
again begin

Spaces wait
faced
in the dark
no waste

Were there
was here
was
always near

Sit down to see
be quiet be
friend
the end

VALENTINE

for Pen

Home's still heart
light in the window
all the familiar
tokens of patience

moved finally out
to let place be
real as it can be
people people

all as they are
and pasteboard red heart
sits there on table
inside the thump bump

passing thought
practical meat
slur and slurp
contracting lump

all for you
wanting a meaning
without you
it would stop

CODA: ROMAN SKETCHBOOK

ROMAN SKETCHBOOK

As you come and go
from a place you sense
the way it might seem
to one truly there as
these clearly determined persons
move on the complex spaces

and hurry to their obvious
or so seeming to you
destinations. "Home," you think,
"is a place still there for all,"
yet now you cannot
simply think it was

or can be the same. It
starts with a small
dislocating ache, the foot
had not been that problem,
but you move nonetheless
and cannot remember the word

for foot, *fuss, pied*? some
thing, a childhood pleasure
she said she could put her
foot in her mouth but
that way is the past again,
someone's, the greying air

looks like evening here, the
traffic moves so densely,
you push close to the walls
of the buildings, the stinking

cars, bikes, people push by.
No fun in being one here,

you have to think. You must
have packed home in mind,
made it up, and yet all
people wait there, still patient
if distracted by what happens.
Out in the night the lights

go on, the shower has cleared the air.
You have a few steps more to the door.
You see it open as you come up, triggered
by its automatic mechanism, a greeting
of sorts, but no one would think of that.
You come in, you walk to the room.

IN THE CIRCLE

In the circle of an
increased limit all
abstracted felt event now

entered at increasing distance
ears hear faintly eye sees
the fading prospects and in-

telligence unable to get the
name back fails and posits
the blank. It largely moves

as a context, habit of being
here as *there* approaches, and
one pulls oneself in to prepare

for the anticipated slight shock—
boat bumping the dock, key
turning in lock, the ticking clock?

APOSTROPHE

Imaginal sharp distances we
push out from, confident
travelers, whose worlds are
specific to bodies—   Realms of
patient existence carried without
thought come to unexpected end
here where nothing waits.

HERE

Back a street is the sunken
pit of the erstwhile market
first century where the feral

cats now wait for something
to fall in and along the
far side is the place where

you get the bus, a broad
street divided by two
areas for standing with a

covered provision, etc. *Antichi*!
Zukofsky'd say—all of it
humbling age, the pitted, pitiful

busts someone's spr——
paint, the small——
with compa——

dank stink floods the evening air.
Where can we go we will not
return to? Each moment, somewhere.

READING/RUSSELL SAYS, "THERE IS
NO RHINOCEROS IN THIS ROOM"

Wittgenstein's insistence to Russell's
equally asserted context of world as
experienced *things* was it's *propositions*
we live in and no "rhinoceros" can
proceed other than fact of what so states
it despite you look under tables or chairs
and open all thinking to prove there's
no rhinoceros here when you've
just brought it in on a plate
of proposed habituated *meaning*
by opening your mouth and out it pops.

ELEVEN AM

Passionate increase of particulars
failing passage to outside formulae
of permitted significance who cry
with foreign eyes out there the
world of all others sky and sun
sudden rain washes the window
air fresh breeze lifts the heavy
curtain to let the room out into
place the street again and people.

James

of a Lady" looking up to
see the frescoes and edging
of baroque seeming ornament
as down on the floor we are

still thinking amid the stacks
of old books and papers, racks,
piles, aisles of patient quiet
again in long, narrow,
pewlike seated halls for
talking sit and think of it.

HOW LONG

How long
to be here
wherever
it is—

I THINK

I think
the steps up
to the flat
parklike top

of hill by the Quirinale look
like where I'd walked when
last here had stopped
before I'd gone in

down to the Coliseum's
huge bulk
the massed rock
and the grassed plot

where the Christians fought
and traffic roars round
as if time
only were mind

or all this
was reminiscence
and what's real
is not.

ROOM

World's become shrunk to
square space high ceiling
box with washed green
sides and mirror the eye
faces to looks to see the
brown haired bent head
red shirt and moving pen
top has place still apparent
whatever else is or was.

OUTSIDE

That curious arrowed sound up
from plazalike street's below
window sun comes in through
small space in vast green drapes
opened for the air and sounds
as one small person's piercing cry.

WALK

Walk out now as if
to the commandment

go forth or is it
come forth   "Come out
with your hands up..."
acquiescent to each step.

WATCHING

Why didn't I call to the
two tense people passing us
sitting at edge of plaza
whom I knew and had reason
to greet but sat watching them
go by with intent nervous faces the
rain just starting as they
went on while I sat with another
friend under large provided umbrella
finishing dregs of the coffee, watching?

VILLA CELIMONTANA

As we walk past crumbling
walls friend's recalling his
first love an American
girl on tour who then
stays for three months in
Rome with him then off
for home and when he
finally gets himself to
New York two years or more
later they go out in
company with her friend
to some place on Broadway
where McCoy Tyner's playing
and now half-loaded comfortable
the friend asks, "What part of

yourself do you express
when you speak English?"
Still thinking of it and me now
as well with *lire* circling my head.

THE STREET

All the various
members of the Italian
Parliament walking
past my lunch!

AS WITH

As with all such
the prospect of ending
gathers now friends take
leave and the afternoon
moves toward the end
of the day. So too mind
moves forward to its place
in time and *now*, one
says, *and now*—

OBJECT

The expandable enveloping flat flesh
he pulls in to center in hotel
room's safety like taking in
the wash which had flapped
all day in the wind. *In*, he
measures his stomach, *in* like
manner his mind, *in*side his

persistent discretion, way, *un*-
opened to anything by *im*pression...

·   ·   ·

So often in such Romantic apprehension
he had wanted only to roam
but howsoever he weighed it or waited
whatsoever was "Rome" was home.

INDEX OF TITLES